The Best of MAC

2000–2009

A Decade of Cartoons from the *Daily Mail*

Stan McMurtry **mac**

Edited by Mark Bryant

PORTICO

For my wonderful wife, Liz

First published in the United Kingdom in 2009 by
Portico
10 Southcombe Street
London
W14 0RA

An imprint of Anova Books Company Ltd.

ISBN 978-1-906032-7-39

A CIP catalogue record for this book is available from the British Library.

10 9 8 7 6 5 4 3 2 1

Printed and bound by WS Bookwell, Finland.

This book can be ordered direct from the publisher at
www.anovabooks.com

Preface

This year it was decided that instead of my annual book of cartoons, which were published in the *Daily Mail* over the past twelve months, a selection of drawings would be gathered together from the past ten years. 'Just pick your favourites,' the publishers said. This was easier said than done. I'm never truly happy with what I drew last week, never mind a whole decade's worth. What should I choose?

On a normal day in my office, after staring at a blank piece of paper for hours, I usually present five rough ideas to the *Daily Mail*'s editor, Paul Dacre, who is very good at sorting the wheat from the chaff. Then off I go back to my drawing-board to produce the finished item. But choosing my own stuff for this book proved tricky. Should I include the quickest cartoon I have ever produced?

This followed the story about the then Deputy Prime Minister, John Prescott, punching an egg-throwing protester in the face. I didn't draw anything at all. A totally blank space appeared in the paper next day with a caption explaining that the cartoon would have been rude about John Prescott and that I didn't want to be thumped by him. I was home early that day.

Anyway it occurred to me that a book of blank pages might not be a bestseller, so I thought it best to include a few drawings. Most of them have my wife, Liz, hidden somewhere in the picture. I hope you enjoy looking for her and the choice of cartoons I have made.

Tory leader William Hague's claims in *GQ* magazine that he drank 14 pints of beer a day as a teenager while working as a delivery man for a drinks company in South Yorkshire were treated with scepticism in some quarters.

'Oh, Norman. I'm so proud. I think our Kevin's going into politics.' *11 August 2000*

After Mike Atherton scored a century at the Oval in the fifth and final test match of the series there was a strong feeling that England could finally beat the West Indies cricket team for the first time in 31 years.

'Doreen, the unbelievable is happening – I think England have a chance of winning the test match!' *4 September 2000*

British Airways suspended 11 short-haul pilots and three cabin crew after they were secretly filmed drinking 'to excess' only hours before flying in a documentary made by Channel 4 TV's *Dispatches* programme.

'Heathrow? Left at the lights, over the bridge, then straight on – but before you go, sir, would you mind blowing into this?' *6 October 2000*

As torrential rain and gale-force winds hit Britain, Republican Governor of Texas George W. Bush clung to a slender advantage over his Democrat rival Al Gore in a stormy contest for election as the next President of the USA.

'The weatherman says it's coming in from across the Atlantic.' *6 November 2000*

The Chancellor's pre-Budget Report gave some concessions to the fuel lobby but angered pensioners when he announced that the basic state pension would only rise by £5 a week (£8 for couples). Meanwhile, Britain suffered its worst floods for 53 years.

'Hurry up, Arnold. A large bottle of cider and 12 packets of crisps. Let's party!' *9 November 2000*

A nationwide survey by the National Pest Technicians' Association revealed a huge increase in the number of brown rats in Britain and reported that a new breed of poison-resistant 'super rats' had begun to spread across the country.

'They don't worry me. Why do you think I've got a dog?' *10 November 2000*

'Don't worry. You've got five seconds' start and if it's not a clean shot my wife wrings your neck.' *20 November 2000*

In the wake of research blaming deep-vein thrombosis and other ailments on cramped seating on aircraft, a House of Lords Select Committee report published new guidelines for the airline industry regarding the health of its passengers.

'Ease up on running on the spot, Betty. You're loosening the wing rivets.' *23 November 2000*

Inspired by the film *Billy Elliot* – in which a working-class boy becomes a star ballet-dancer – Education Secretary David Blunkett pledged £35 million to fund after-school classes in dance, drama and music for deprived inner-city children.

'Aye. I'm bloody ashamed of him. He wants to be a miner.' *13 February 2001*

With the confirmation of the first major outbreak of foot-and-mouth disease in the country for 20 years, supermarkets and butchers began to run out of meat and there were fears of huge price increases as shops were forced to buy in stocks from overseas.

'Nut cutlets again! Surely there must be some meat in the house we can eat?' *2 March 2001*

In an effort to prevent the spread of further contagion, Agriculture Minister Nick Brown announced that the Army might have to be called in to control the ever-worsening foot-and-mouth crisis.

'Marjorie. Some people are here about your sore foot.' *13 March 2001*

Prince Edward and Sophie – who had referred to the Queen as 'the old dear' – were summoned to Buckingham Palace after it was claimed that they were using tax-payer-funded state visits to drum up business for Edward's ailing TV company Ardent.

'Edward. Can you and Sophie pop round again? The old dear would like another word.' *6 April 2001*

Speculation that 71-year-old Great Train Robber Ronnie Biggs, who had suffered three strokes, would be allowed to return to the UK from Brazil after 35 years on compassionate grounds proved justified.

'I know it's hard after all this time, Lucan. But I may have to let you go.' *4 May 2001*

Deputy Prime Minister John Prescott punched a countryside protester in the face and became involved in a brawl after he was hit by an egg on his way to address a meeting in Rhyl, North Wales.

mac

This cartoon was going to poke fun at John Prescott. But I want to keep my teeth – Mac. *18 May 2001*

Scotland Yard announced that it would be issuing 'Taser' electronic stun guns to the police by Christmas. The US-made guns use laser-targeted darts to deliver a 50,000-volt shock capable of temporarily paralysing victims and have a range of 20 feet.

'Golly gosh, Sarge. You're pretty fast. Another split second and he would have fouled the pavement.' *2 August 2001*

After the Home Office recommended that speed cameras should be painted orange the Chief Constable of Norfolk added on BBC Radio 4's *Today* programme that more warnings should be given about their location to encourage drivers to slow down.

'You'd have thought painting them orange would've been enough.' *3 August 2001*

French police reported that they had eventually captured 44 asylum-seekers who had managed to walk seven miles into the Channel Tunnel.

'Quickly, Mohammad. Quickly! Put another leaf on the line.' *3 September 2001*

After an outbreak of the killer virus anthrax in Boca Raton, Florida, USA, the British Government revealed that it only had enough stock of the anti-anthrax drug doxycycline to treat two million people.

'Don't drink that one, mother. It's our anti-anthrax vaccine.' *16 October 2001*

An appeal court decided that Tony Martin, the 56-year-old Norfolk farmer convicted of killing a teenage burglar, should serve a further year in prison. Meanwhile, the burglar's accomplice walked free after serving only part of his three-year sentence.

'Good evening, sir. These gentlemen are here to ransack your house. I must warn you that any attempt by you to resist entry could result in a long prison sentence...' *1 November 2001*

As US-led forces bombed the Taliban's last remaining stronghold in the Tora Bora caves in southern Afghanistan there was still no sign of Osama bin Laden, who was later believed by many to have been smuggled into neighbouring Pakistan.

'I bet he's shaved off his beard and slipped into Pakistan or somewhere that's easy to get in to.' *17 December 2001*

After finally admitting that ever-increasing street-crime had made Britain's cities unsafe, Home Secretary David Blunkett introduced a six-month Robbery Reduction Initiative in which 5000 police officers would be transferred back on to the beat.

'Of course, it takes a bit longer to get to the shops but at least you don't get mugged.' *19 March 2002*

After Culture Secretary Tessa Jowell introduced a White Paper proposing the relaxation on casino-licensing and gambling – thereby earning the Government £1.5 billion a year in tax – developers planned to make Blackpool the gambling capital of Europe.

'Tell y'what. Let's have one more go at this daft kid's game then all pop next door for bingo and a bacon buttie.' *28 March 2002*

There were fears for passenger safety when a major computer glitch at the National Air Traffic Control System – the second within two weeks – caused widespread chaos and the delay or cancellation of 700 UK flights affecting 150,000 air travellers.

'We apologise to passengers for the severe delays. Rest assured our engineers are working flat out to trace the computer fault...' *11 April 2002*

A 27-year-old male streaker from North Shields, with 'Rude Britannia' tattooed on his buttocks, ran beside the Queen's car for 50 yards as she drove to St Mary's Cathedral, Newcastle upon Tyne, to unveil a statue in honour of the late Cardinal Basil Hume.

'There was a streaker? Goodness me, I must be getting old. I didn't notice.' *9 May 2002*

As two hostile neighbours, India and Pakistan, threatened a nuclear holocaust over Kashmir, the only focus of British media attention was on whether England skipper David Beckham's injured foot would heal in time for the start of the 2002 World Cup.

'Have you got anything on the Pakistan-India nuclear threat?' *28 May 2002*

The celebrations to mark the Queen's Golden Jubilee included classical and pop music concerts at Buckingham Palace. Among those performing in the pop concert were Sir Cliff Richard, Sir Elton John and Tom Jones.

'Do stop fidgeting, Philip. I'm told it will be expected of one to throw undergarments at Tom Jones when he sings tonight.'

3 June 2002

'Excuse me. if you're Arabella Pilkington-Smythe, formerly Arthur Finkley, who's £435.20 in the red, been married three times and has two moles on her right buttock – you've dropped your ID card.' *2 July 2002*

A report in the *New Scientist* revealed that a joint study by researchers at the University of Lincoln and the University of Minas Gerais in Brazil had shown that dogs can count and that their barking is more like a language than previously supposed.

''Don't look like that. I've only had two pints.' *2 August 2002*

As A-level results hit a new high with a pass-rate of 94.3% and predictions of a 100% pass-rate by 2004, many employers and universities argued that the examinations were getting easier and that they were no longer a useful measure of ability.

'90 per cent of me wants to go out and celebrate, but the other 50 per cent asks: Were they dumbing down?' *15 August 2002*

Britain's long diplomatic silence over the enforced evictions of white farmers in Zimbabwe was finally broken after the USA publicly condemned the practice and declared that it did not recognise President Robert Mugabe as the country's legitimate leader.

'Oh. Er...right then. I condemn Mugabe too!' *23 August 2002*

Britain was put on a war footing as Prime Minister Tony Blair flew to the USA for talks on Iraq with President Bush. Meanwhile, a record number of asylum-seekers in Britain – predominantly from Iraq and Afghanistan – led to a huge backlog in the processing of applications.

'Don't worry. By the time they've processed our asylum applications the bombing will be over and we can go home.'

3 September 2002

A Japanese company announced that it had developed a translation system called Bow-Lingual which it claimed could convert the barks, howls and whines of dogs into human language.

'You heard me. You've got ten minutes. If you're not back from the pub and opening a can of Doggydins by then the cat goes in the microwave!' *11 October 2002*

'Another half pint? Don't be silly. I've got to drive home for breakfast in a couple of hours' time.' *15 November 2002*

Prime Minister Tony Blair's leadership seemed to be in jeopardy as a million peace protesters marched through London to demonstrate against Britain going to war with Iraq, and many senior members of the Labour Party threatened to resign.

'Okay, everybody. Keep in line!' *17 February 2003*

New rules introduced by Home Secretary David Blunkett to curb bogus asylum-seekers, by denying benefits to those who fail to claim asylum as soon as they enter Britain, were declared illegal by the High Court.

'Sometimes, Sadie, I feel you're the only one I can trust – you wouldn't be letting in every down-on-their-luck asylum-seeker...'

20 February 2003

The war in Iraq was the first 'media war' in which there was non-stop live TV coverage by broadcasters on both sides of the conflict.

'War, war, war! Is anything else on the other channel?' *25 March 2003*

There was considerable legal controversy when a surrogate mother from Sunderland decided that she wanted to take back the baby girl she had given birth to, *just six days after handing her over to her future parents.*

'I just hope his surrogate mother won't mind having him back after all these years.' *22 April 2003*

A scientific study based on information gathered by 900 researchers investigating 'ghostly feelings' at famous haunted sites claimed that these could be explained by environmental factors such as tiny changes in light, temperature, smell and magnetic fields.

'Quiet, please. One question at a time. – You, sir, the man in the third row with his head under his arm...' *22 May 2003*

Britain seemed to be moving ever closer to Europe. However, on the issue of the single currency, Chancellor Gordon Brown's long-awaited 1700-page report – published after six years of study by Treasury experts – concluded 'Not Yet'.

'Nearly there...wait for it...wait for it...' *10 June 2003*

Britain's Number 1 tennis-player, Tim Henman, was defeated by Frenchman Sebastien Grosjean
in the Wimbledon quarter-finals.

'How did Tim Henman get on?' *4 July 2003*

Millionaire novelist Jeffrey Archer was released from prison after serving two years and two days of a four-year sentence for perjury and perverting the course of justice after faking an alibi in a libel case involving the prostitute Monica Coghlan.

'Jeffrey. You're home now! There's no bucket.' *22 July 2003*

There was considerable controversy when Anglican leaders in the USA elected Canon Gene Robinson, an openly gay priest, as bishop of New Hampshire.

'...and how was your holiday in America, Vicar?' *7 August 2003*

As the number of speed cameras increased throughout Britain, there was widespread criticism of police priorities, especially when it was revealed that police in Scarborough, Yorkshire, had taken two and a half hours to respond to a 999 call.

'Sorry for the delay in answering your 999 call, madam. This is due to us being absolutely overwhelmed by paperwork.'
19 August 2003

Deputy Prime Minister John Prescott overruled the decision of an independent planning inquiry and approved the construction of a giant country camp for 750 asylum-seekers in Bicester, Oxfordshire, despite widespread local opposition.

'We've been refused planning permission for a car port again. They say it would be unsightly.' *21 August 2003*

'Aw, come on, Bernard. It's past midnight. Let him come in for his tea.' *25 November 2003*

An inventor in the USA planned to market an electronic device which gave women orgasms at the touch of a button. It was nicknamed the Orgasmatron after a similar fictional machine in Woody Allen's futuristic film, *Sleeper*.

'What d'you mean you've got a headache?' *28 November 2003*

An all-party select committee of peers and MPs met to scrutinise a new draft Gambling Bill which many feared would allow Las Vegas-style casinos to be set up on every high street in Britain.

'I take it our usual Friday night game of rummy is off?' *8 April 2004*

A warehouse fire in East London wiped out works of art valued at millions of pounds.
Amongst the items destroyed was a collection belonging to Charles Saatchi which
included works by Tracey Emin, the Chapman Brothers and Damien Hirst.

'Charles Saatchi is a genius! Last time I looked in here it was just a collection of pretentious old tat.' *27 May 2004*

As almost 12 years had passed since his separation from Princess Diana and it was nearly seven years since her death, the former Archbishop of Canterbury, Lord Carey, said that Prince Charles should make an 'honest woman' of Camilla Parker Bowles.

'Thank you, Parker. Now pop upstairs, drop romantically down on one knee and ask Camilla if she'll consent to be my wife.'

3 June 2004

There was much public confusion over the experimental postal voting system for the local and European elections introduced in certain parts of Britain, with many ballot papers not being delivered in time and reports of electoral fraud and intimidation.

'Even now some people are still very confused about postal voting.' *10 June 2004*

English soccer hooligans rioted in Albufeira, Portugal, in the run-up to the UEFA Euro 2004 group match against Switzerland. Meanwhile, new research claimed that stem cells could be used to create brain cells to replace tissue damaged by Parkinson's Disease and strokes.

'Strange isn't it? Since meeting those blokes from the stem-cell research unit who can make brain tissue, I've had an overwhelming urge to curl up with a good book.' *17 June 2004*

Lord Butler's report into the reasons for the Iraq war – during which 11,500 civilians and 60 British soldiers were killed – condemned the false intelligence over Saddam's alleged weapons of mass destruction but refused to blame any individuals.

'Guess what, everyone? Nobody's to blame.' *15 July 2004*

A report by Adair Turner, head of the Government's Pensions Commission, said that to plug the £57 billion black hole in public and private pensions provision, men and women would have to delay their retirement ages to 70 and 67, respectively.

'Damn! He's got away!' *14 October 2004*

At a ceremony in Balaclava, Ukraine, to mark the 150th anniversary of the Charge of the Light Brigade, the 83-year-old Duke of Edinburgh wore sunglasses to cover up a black eye he claimed was the result of a fall in the bathroom of his hotel.

'I'll tell everyone he slipped in the bath. But I'm warning you, Harry – don't you dare take your grandfather nightclubbing again!'

27 October 2004

Plans unveiled in the Government's Children Bill would mean that parents caught smacking their children severely enough to mark the skin could face up to five years in jail. Meanwhile, the crucial final debate on hunting with hounds approached.

'I think it's instead of smacking.' *3 November 2004*

Environmental campaigners and rural communities were shocked when Deputy Prime Minister John Prescott announced plans to build a further 130,000 new homes across the South East of England at a time when thousands of properties stood empty in the area.

'Sadly, since John Prescott took all our land for housing, Bernard's thinking seriously about getting out of farming.'
10 November 2004

The Government announced plans to introduce compulsory identity cards to help guard against terrorism. Meanwhile, Buckingham Palace's security was tightened after another fathers' rights protester scaled a 20-foot gatepost and chained himself to it.

'Come on, come on. How are we to know you're not Al Qaeda? – Where's your ID card?' *24 November 2004*

Home Secretary David Blunkett launched a legal bid to prove that he was the father of his pregnant former lover's baby and her two-year-old son, and threatened to give up his Cabinet post to fight for access to the children he believed were his.

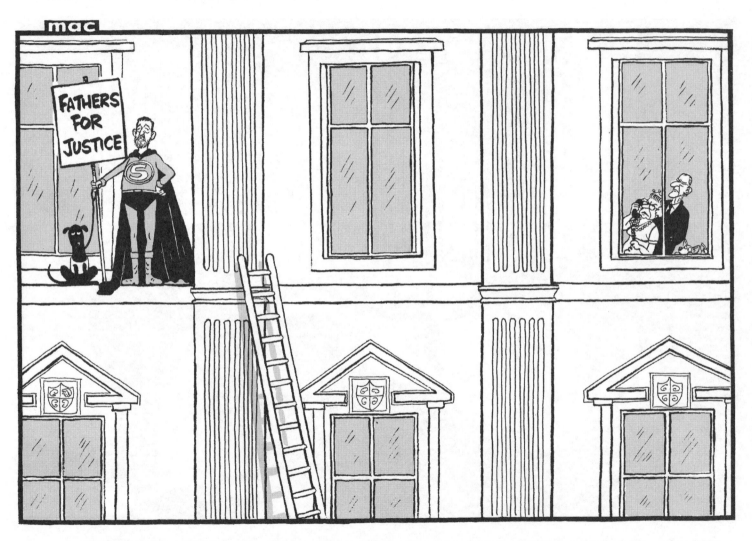

'Mr Blair. Will you kindly come and remove your Home Secretary from my window ledge?' *2 December 2004*

'Air Miles Andy' faced a ban on using tax-payers' money for private trips when an official report from the National Audit Office revealed that Prince Andrew had spent £325,000 in a single year on hiring aircraft to fly to golf matches and other events.

'Could you move your buggy back a bit, Prince Andrew? It's on my ball.' *25 January 2005*

After much discussion it was agreed that after their marriage Prince Charles's wife would be addressed as HRH the Duchess of Cornwall, but it was still unclear whether she would become Queen if and when Prince Charles accedes to the throne.

'It's your mother, sir. Did Mrs Parker Bowles accidentally pick up the wrong hat when you last visited?' *15 February 2005*

In an attempt to stem rising school drop-out rates and improve literacy, Chancellor Gordon Brown unveiled new Education Maintenance Allowances of £75 a week to encourage youngsters to stay in full-time education or training.

'I bet it says fags are up again.' *17 March 2005*

Prince Charles and Camilla Parker Bowles were married at the Guildhall, Windsor, on 9 April 2005. Following a risk-assessment study on his new wife, the Duchess of Cornwall was given a new SAS-trained female police bodyguard.

'Charles, dear. Would you tell Camilla that her in-laws have popped in for a cup of tea and to mention this to her new bodyguard?' *27 April 2005*

Royal Ascot was moved to York to allow the racecourse to be redeveloped.

'Oh. You don't understand one's accent? – Try this: By 'eck, lad. T'bugger coom in fust.
Fifty smackers or ah'll set t'corgi on tha!' *16 June 2005*

Bow Street Magistrates Court heard how a young hacker from North London, working from his bedroom, gained access to nearly 100 US Government computers, including those at the Pentagon and NASA as well as the US Army and Navy.

'I'm warning you, Nigel. If you try sending the American fleet to nuke Russia again you'll go to bed without any tea.' *29 July 2005*

Aged 62, wrinkly rocker Sir Mick Jagger and the Rolling Stones kicked off their latest world tour – estimated to earn them £10 million each – with a sell-out concert at Boston's Fenway Park baseball stadium.

'I think I've pulled. Mick's asked me back to his place for cocoa and a digestive biscuit.' *24 August 2005*

For the first time in many years, Australia's cricket team found themselves trailing badly to England in the annual Test Match, with only one match left to play to win the Ashes.

'Come on now, Bruce. Show you're a good loser. Take our Pom neighbour a beer and apologise for shearing him and nailing him to the shed.' *30 August 2005*

There was widespread jubilation amongst cricket fans as England beat
Australia and won the Ashes for the first time in 18 years.

'I've washed that ugly old egg-cup thing. It was full of ashes.' *14 September 2005*

As a killer bird flu virus reached Romania from Turkey, Britain's Chief Medical Officer, Sir Liam Donaldson, warned that if it was able to cross over into humans there could be a pandemic, with as many as 50,000 victims in the UK alone.

'This is a raid, buster! Hand over the parrot food or I sneeze!' *18 October 2005*

The latest official police figures revealed that violent crime was up by 6% in England and Wales. Much of the increase was blamed on binge drinking.

'Before we go in, I'd like to apologise profusely for beating you to a pulp when we come out.' *21 October 2005*

As the debate over the wisdom of allowing 24-hour drinking continued, the Government introduced a 'Britishness' test for immigrants who wished to apply for a British passport.

'Congratulations, Mr Sajeed. You've passed the Government's Britishness test.' *1 November 2005*

Prime Minister Tony Blair was at the centre of a 'cash for honours' scandal when leaked documents revealed that 18 millionaires who had donated a total of £16 million to Labour Party funds over the past nine years had been given peerages.

'Sorry, lads. I can't buy a round. I've just sent my last twenty quid to Tony Blair.' *9 November 2005*

The Queen celebrated her 80th birthday. She received more than 20,000 birthday cards.

'If that's the post, Philip dear, will you see if there are any cards for me?' *21 April 2006*

Health Secretary Patricia Hewitt faced a furious backlash after claiming that 'despite the headlines the NHS has just had its best year yet'. Meanwhile, a report by the Royal College of Nursing said there had been 13,000 redundancies since October.

'That's a relief. It's all just an exaggeration by the newspapers, according to Patricia Hewitt.' *25 April 2006*

The overweight Deputy PM John Prescott hit the headlines when he admitted he had used his official residences – funded by the taxpayer – to carry on an affair with his diary secretary. Later two other women also claimed to have had relationships with him.

'Those poor women. Imagine what it must be like sleeping with John Prescott.' *2 May 2006*

It was announced that a Sussex woman, who would be 63 in September, was seven months pregnant after receiving fertility treatment in Italy.

'Damn! Have you ever walked into a room then forgotten what you came in for?' *5 May 2006*

In a deal worth £10 billion, the Spanish construction firm Ferrovial bought British Airports Authority (BAA), owner of seven UK airports including Heathrow and Gatwick.

'You must admit he's much more fun than the man with the ping-pong bats.' *7 June 2006*

The Institution of Civil Engineers proposed the establishment of a national grid for water – similar to those for gas and electricity – with pipelines diverting water from the River Trent, Wales and the North to prevent shortages in London and the South.

'Stanley hates Southerners.' *28 June 2006*

The National Farmers' Union and a number of academics backed claims made by West Country cheesemakers that cows moo with regional accents depending of which part of Britain they live in.

'Thanks for the elocution lessons but I think I preferred them mooing with a Brummie accent.' *24 August 2006*

A 31-year-old Iraqi man who lost his sight in a bomb-blast in his homeland became the first blind person in the UK to be convicted of dangerous driving. Arrested in the West Midlands he had been given instructions on braking and turning by a passenger.

'Okay, relax. It isn't that blind bloke driving again. It's his guide dog.' *6 September 2006*

Opposition MPs demanded that British troops serving in Iraq and Afghanistan should be given the same tax breaks as their foreign allies when it was pointed out that US troops are exempt from paying tax while stationed in a theatre of war.

'Young man. There appears to be a small discrepancy in your last tax return.' *3 October 2006*

In a major breakthrough in stem-cell research which could revolutionise the future of organ transplants, British scientists at Newcastle University announced that they had produced the world's first ever laboratory-grown human liver.

'Thanks for leaving me that bit of liver last night. It went down a treat with the onions and gravy.' *1 November 2006*

A 55-year-old British Airways employee who had worn a tiny Christian cross around her neck to work for seven years took the airline to court over its new regulations which insisted that all personal items should be worn under the BA uniform.

'Y'know, British Airways are right. A cross does look better worn under the uniform.' *22 November 2006*

In what many saw as a further extension of the 'Big Brother' culture, a new scheme was introduced in which all motorists pulled over by the police would be fingerprinted at the roadside to check their identity against the 6.5 million recorded prints of crime suspects.

'Good Lord, Marjorie. Is this true? Your prints match those found at the Brink's-Mat bullion heist 23 years ago.' *23 November 2006*

Speaking to the Council of Foreign Relations think-tank in New York, Iraq's Vice-President Tareq Al-Hashemi claimed that Tony Blair had set a timetable for pulling British troops out of Iraq but that George Bush had 'brainwashed' him into changing his mind.

'Gee, George, honey. Why's Tony doing backward flips outside Downing Street in his underpants?' *21 December 2006*

'How terribly exciting, Philip, dear. They're making a film called *Helen Mirren* and I've been offered the part.' *17 January 2007*

A new biography of Conservative Party leader David Cameron revealed that he had been disciplined at Eton for smoking cannabis at the age of 15.

'Dashed if I know what Cameron saw in this stuff. Does nothing for me ... my God, you're beautiful!' *13 February 2007*

Shortly before he was due to be posted to Iraq, 22-year-old Prince Harry was reprimanded by superior officers in his regiment, the Blues & Royals, after a series of incidents in which he was found to be drunk and disorderly in public places.

'Oh really? Well I brought my granny along too and we both think your conduct has been appalling!' *3 April 2007*

In the local council elections the Labour Party suffered its worst defeat in 35 years. Amongst the casualties were many of the Labour-run local authorities which had introduced fortnightly refuse collections.

'Now they've been voted out, do we collect them this week or in a fortnight?' *4 May 2007*

At a historic ceremony in Stormont Castle, Belfast, the Rev. Ian Paisley, leader of the Democratic Unionist Party, became First Minister of Northern Ireland's new devolved power-sharing government with Sinn Féin's Martin McGuinness as his deputy.

New Friends? *9 May 2007*

The head of the British Army, General Sir Richard Dannatt, ruled that Prince Harry could not serve in Iraq as he would be a prime target for snipers and hostage-takers. There were suggestions that he might serve in Afghanistan instead.

'Well, chaps, here we are. Front line, Afghanistan and ... oh, good shot, your Royal Highness!' *18 May 2007*

The latest figures published by the Healthcare Commission watchdog as part of its annual 'health check' revealed that a quarter of the 394 English NHS Trusts had breached the Hygiene Code for hospitals introduced last October.

'Nurse! The rats have got old Ferguson again!' *19 June 2007*

At his last Prime Minister's Question Time, Tony Blair was given an unprecedented standing ovation by Labour and Tory MPs. Meanwhile, a monsoon-like downpour led to widespread flooding as more rain fell in 24 hours than the average for the whole of June.

'... and so, as a fitting end to his ten glorious years, Tony Blair walks triumphantly off into the sunset...' *28 June 2007*

Massive downpours caused chaos, with three months of rain falling in a few hours in some parts of the country. In Tewkesbury, Gloucestershire, flooding left 350,000 people without drinking water when a treatment plant became contaminated.

'Oh, you poor things. How have you managed without drinking water?' *24 July 2007*

A judge in Manchester condemned police for wasting tax-payers' money when it was revealed in court that a 12-year-old boy, who had thrown a cocktail sausage at a pensioner during an argument, had been arrested and charged with common assault.

'Be careful, Sarge. He's got a sausage!' *24 August 2007*

Research published in *The Lancet* by scientists working for the Government's Food Standards Agency found that artificial additives in children's food – especially colourings in sweets, biscuits, soft drinks and ice-cream – can affect their behaviour.

'That was delicious, mummy. Don't worry, I'll do the dishes, then I think I'll tidy my room and curl up in bed with my book on Scouting.' *7 September 2007*

When Chancellor Alistair Darling admitted that two HM Revenue & Customs computer discs containing personal and banking details of 25 million Child Benefit claimants had gone missing in the post there were nationwide worries about the risk of identity fraud.

'Good heavens, Mavis. It's you! This woman must have stolen your identity!' *22 November 2007*

Young women invited to Manchester United's Christmas party held at an exclusive £395-a-night hotel in the city complained that they had been treated like 'pieces of meat' by some of the players.

'That's the last Manchester United party I go to – they treat you like a piece of meat.' *20 December 2007*

When a 68-year-old animal behaviourist from East Sussex developed crippling arthritis in her back, she trained her Newfoundland dog to work the washing-machine, help with housework and carry shopping bags.

'... and another thing. Next door's dog does the laundry, tidies up and brings the shopping home!' *4 January 2008*

Schools Secretary Ed Balls announced that all secondary-school pupils aged between 11 and 14 would be given practical cookery lessons in an effort to combat obesity and to encourage teenagers to eat healthy meals instead of relying on processed foods.

'You were asked to bring two sardines and a carrot, Munshmore. Giant beefburgers and chips are out.' *23 January 2008*

A survey conducted by the *Daily Mail* revealed that 63 MPs admitted to employing relatives to help them with their parliamentary business.

'In view of current investigations I'm afraid I can no longer keep you on as my parliamentary assistant, mother.' *31 January 2008*

Britain's second largest earthquake in the past decade, measuring 4.7 on the Richter scale, shook most of England from Durham to the Home Counties.

'Honestly. I'd just finished tidying my room when there was this huge earth tremor.' *28 February 2008*

Reports by the Royal Institution of Chartered Surveyors and others revealed that the housing market was at its worst for 30 years with one in three estate agents facing closure within the next twelve months.

'Oh yes. I come down here most mornings to feed the estate agents.' *15 April 2008*

A report by insurance companies revealed that thefts from gardens had doubled over the past twelve months. As well as statues and garden furniture, expensive plants, trees, shrubs and even whole lawns had been uprooted.

'Keep a close eye on my azaleas. Apparently garden thefts are on the increase.' *7 May 2008*

Robert Mugabe, President of Zimbabwe for the past 28 years, was returned to power after escalating violence against supporters of Morgan Tsvangirai, leader of the Movement for Democratic Change, forced him to withdraw from the final stages of the election.

24 June 2008

Just days after a memory stick containing details of nearly 130,000 criminals went missing from the Home Office, personal details of more than a million bank customers were discovered on the hard drive of a computer sold on eBay.

'Here's an unusual one, Wayne. Gentleman says he's lost an umbrella.' *27 August 2008*

Works by Damien Hirst, including The Golden Calf, featuring the preserved
corpse of a real calf, were auctioned by Sotheby's in London.

'Well I think Sotheby's will spot it's a forgery – it's still got the batter on it.' *18 September 2008*

A series of new educational videos published by the Women's Institute for its members included documentaries on gardening, home management and sex tips for women over 50.

'To be honest, Enid, the video would spice up our sex life a lot more if you weren't making marmalade at the same time.'
15 October 2008

In Barcelona, Spain, a 30-year-old mother became the first person in the world to undergo a transplant using a whole organ grown from her own stem cells.

'We're doing our best, Mr Winsborrow. But you have to remember, stem-cell research is still in its infancy...'

20 November 2008

After a century of trading in the UK, high-street retailer Woolworths plc went into administration, closing 815 shops with the loss of 25,000 jobs.

'I can't wait to see your Dad's face on Christmas Day... I've bought him Woolworths.' *28 November 2008*

There was considerable optimism worldwide when the 47-year-old Democrat
Barack Hussein Obama II became the 44th President of the USA.

'Shucks, Michelle. It's never happened before. I can walk on it but I can't get in it.' *22 January 2009*

British scientists cast doubt on claims made by a US Professor in a documentary in BBC2's *Horizon* series which suggested that obesity could be caught like a common cold from overweight people carrying the highly infectious adenovirus.

'Honestly, darling, it's me...I was standing next to a fat woman in Tesco's and she sneezed.' *27 January 2009*

Public anger ran high when it was revealed that sacked top executives at failed banks rescued using taxpayers' money had received massive payoffs. Meanwhile, an official report said that infestation by rats and other vermin in Britain was at record levels.

'It's true – apparently you are never more than ten feet from a banker.' *11 February 2009*

'I felt sorry for the British. After all the glitz and glamour they had to return to the poverty and debt back home.' *24 February 2009*

Prime Minister Gordon Brown arrived in Washington for talks with President Obama on how to combat the international banking crisis. Meanwhile, Robert Mugabe remained as President of Zimbabwe as his own country's economy spiralled out of control.

'Let's see now. Apart from corrupt bankers and politicians your country is broke, yet you're still clinging to power – how can I help you, Mr Mugabe?' *3 March 2009*

With interest rates at an all-time low the Bank of England announced a programme of 'quantitative easing' by pumping £75 billion into the banking system to stimulate economic growth. Many saw this as simply printing money.

'Can I take a message? He's busy on a programme of quantitative easing to kick start the economy.' *6 March 2009*

On his first ever official visit to Europe, President Obama arrived in London amidst tight security for the G20 economic summit. A dinner was also held in his honour at 10 Downing Street, hosted by Gordon Brown.

'Aw, come on! Surely you Yanks have heard of April Fool?' *1 April 2009*

When the *Daily Telegraph* revealed that a number of MPs had made illegal claims for expenses on their second homes, the *Daily Mail* joined forces with the Tax Payers' Alliance to campaign for the private prosecution of those found guilty.

'...and then in 2009 a massive second home for all MPs was built – it was called "jail".' *15 May 2009*

63-year-old Glaswegian Michael Martin MP, nicknamed 'Gorbals Mick', was forced to resign as Speaker of the House of Commons – the first to have been ousted from the job in more than 300 years.

'Orders...Orders!' *20 May 2009*

The *Daily Telegraph* revealed that a Conservative MP had claimed £1600 to construct a floating island – complete with a miniature house modelled on an 18th-century Swedish building – on a lake in his Hampshire home to keep his ducks safe from foxes.

'Make the most of this. Our man is being forced to stand down at the next election.' *22 May 2009*

More revelations about MPs abusing their expenses allowances appeared in the press, with one Tory grandee even claiming £17,000 for servants' quarters in his six-bedroom country house in Woking, Surrey.

'Please apologise to the rest of the staff in there, Benskins. But you know I can't claim for servants' quarters any more.' *29 May 2009*

The expenses row, coupled with expected bad results for Labour in the local and European elections, led to the resignation of Home Secretary Jacqui Smith and a number of other Cabinet ministers.

'Mrs Perkins. How would you like to be Home Secretary?' *3 June 2009*

The official record of MPs' expenses was finally published, with huge sections blacked out by Government censors. Meanwhile, it was announced that the results of the long-awaited Iraq war inquiry would not be published until after the next general election.

19 June 2009